# Questions for Kids

To Penny

I hope this book facilitates some great family dialogue!

*[signature]*
8/17

# Questions for Kids

THE TIME TO START TALKING
WITH KIDS IS NOW!

• • •

*Jon Pollock*

© 2017 Jon Pollock
All rights reserved.

ISBN-13: 9781547153121
ISBN-10: 1547153121
Library of Congress Control Number: 2017908984
CreateSpace Independent Publishing Platform
North Charleston, South Carolina

**If you want to learn, test, or teach anything, just ask the right questions.**

During a lunch visit with good friends, Jerry Koch and Bruce Crocombe were among the first non-family members to hear about the questions we had recently asked our grandkids. They asked for copies of the questions to try out with their own families. After reporting back about the wonderful dialogue that resulted, they each asked for more questions. Their experience and encouragement prompted the creation of what you now hold in your hands.

When about 300 questions had been compiled, I contacted another friend who had actually published several novels about Africa. Rory Johnston actually knows some of our grandkids and was kind enough to listen to my elevator pitch. He read through the questions and felt this was truly a unique concept that should be brought to market.

Lists of questions alone, however, would not work. He suggested dividing the questions into topical categories and providing introductions for each section. Rory also put me in touch with his publishing consultant, Gaines Hill, who is with CreateSpace. The staff of this Amazon based company have been excellent to work with and ultimately enabled me to self-publish this book in a matter of months.

Once the manuscript was farther along, another good friend who is also an experienced author agreed to read it and provide comments. Alan Spector was a wonderful resource who taught me quite a lot. He asked excellent questions, offered constructive criticism, and challenged me to make it even better. Where would anyone be without friends? Alan, I am forever in your debt.

This book would surely have been possible without my wife, but it would not have been nearly as good. For the last half century, we have loved, learned, shared, fought, supported, survived, and literally grown up together. Not many twenty-year-olds are as fortunate as we were to have married and survived the daily assault we refer to as life. Was this luck, fate, or something else? After being together for fifty years, we are still trying to figure it out.

Without question, Janie is my best friend, my staunchest supporter, and my toughest critic. She keeps me well-grounded and aware of what is going on around us while making sure that I look presentable at nearly all times. Thankfully, one of us has good taste.

We are fiercely proud of our children. While our three adult kids share a family bond, they are each strong and independent in their own individual ways. We have instilled in them the same work ethic and core values that were important to us. And now, they are passing these same characteristics on to our seven grandkids.

This book is therefore dedicated to our future:

**Jacob, Bryce, Tyler, Marin, Avery, Leighton, and Grahm**

May you never stop asking questions and helping those around you to find all of the many answers.

With all my love,
Poppy
(AKA Jon Pollock)
May 23, 2017

MyQuestionsForKids@gmail.com
www.MyQuestionsForKids.com

# Forward

• • •

PART OF WALT DISNEY'S GENIUS is that he created an environment that was ostensibly for kids, but did so in a way in which the parents also had a magical experience. My wife and I took our kids to Disneyland or Disney World about every three to four years as they were growing up, but we've also been there a couple of times on our own since our daughter and son left the nest.

In *Questions for Kids*, Jon Pollock has emulated Disney. He has created an approach that engages our children and grandchildren in the Socratic Method to stimulate their critical thinking by asking them important questions and giving them the space to answer and defend their points of view without judgement. As Jon guides us, "There is no right or wrong answer." Rather, it is the excitement of the open dialogue that is the power of Jon's questions.

But while the approach is focused on the kids, Jon engages the adults as well by using social commentary to provide us with the essence of a parenting and grand-parenting manual. Each chapter delves into a different subject, providing guidance as to why it is important and historical perspective to help us understand the matter more deeply. Then comes the multitude of questions he has collected from which we can choose which to ask our kids. But, yes, the questions are thought provoking for us as well.

In 1963, my high school class elected Jon Pollock to be our Senior Class President. We did so because even then, we recognized he cared for others, had a solid foundation of personal values, was deeply intelligent, and made everyone around him better for having known him. More than five decades later, Jon continues to exhibit these traits, and they are in full bloom in this insightful book. Oh, by the way, Jon's election was also enabled by winning the senior class female vote, because all of the girls thought he was cute—it was a high school thing.

Does Jon still care about others? You will see that he is profoundly committed to the well-being of his family, and this book is exhibit one that he also cares about us as he shares what his family has learned to our benefit.

Does Jon still have a solid foundation of deep personal values? His thoughtful treatment of each chapter's topics is evidence that the answer is "Yes."

Is Jon still deeply intelligent? He not only shares his well-reasoned points of view, but he builds those points from a studied perspective.

Does Jon still make the people around him better for just having known him? I'm confident that you'll feel that he has made a positive difference for you and that he's created an approach to enable you to influence your children and grandchildren in a profound way.

Is Jon still cute? That, I'm sorry, is not for me to say.

*Questions for Kids* is an innovative way to get our kids away from their screens and into a conversation. The book is also provocative and instructive for each of us, whether we agree with Jon's points of view or not. Remarkably, Jon has integrated three achievements into one holistic message—an approach to help our children and grandchildren grow, a thought-provoking social commentary, and a parenting/grand-parenting manual.

How will your children answer Jon's questions? And importantly, how would you answer them?

Alan Spector

Author at www.aaspector.com

Proud grandparent of four

# Contents

Forward · · · · · · · · · · · · · · · · · · · · · · · · · · · · · · · · · · · · · · · · · · vii
Introduction · · · · · · · · · · · · · · · · · · · · · · · · · · · · · · · · · · · · · · · · xi

Questions About You · · · · · · · · · · · · · · · · · · · · · · · · · · · · · · · · · 1
Questions About Peers · · · · · · · · · · · · · · · · · · · · · · · · · · · · · · · 20
Family Questions · · · · · · · · · · · · · · · · · · · · · · · · · · · · · · · · · · · 30
Questions About Social Media · · · · · · · · · · · · · · · · · · · · · · · 39
Questions About Education · · · · · · · · · · · · · · · · · · · · · · · · · 46
Questions About Beliefs · · · · · · · · · · · · · · · · · · · · · · · · · · · · 56
Questions About Authority · · · · · · · · · · · · · · · · · · · · · · · · · 66
Questions About Sports · · · · · · · · · · · · · · · · · · · · · · · · · · · · 71
Questions About Money · · · · · · · · · · · · · · · · · · · · · · · · · · · 79
Questions About Government · · · · · · · · · · · · · · · · · · · · · · 88
Questions About Business · · · · · · · · · · · · · · · · · · · · · · · · · 100
Extended Discussions · · · · · · · · · · · · · · · · · · · · · · · · · · · · · 110

Postscript · · · · · · · · · · · · · · · · · · · · · · · · · · · · · · · · · · · · · · · · 115
About the Author · · · · · · · · · · · · · · · · · · · · · · · · · · · · · · · · · 117

# Introduction

● ● ●

*The children now love luxury; they have bad manners, contempt for authority; they show disrespect for elders and love chatter in place of exercise. Children are now tyrants, not the servants of their households. They no longer rise when elders enter the room. They contradict their parents, chatter before company, gobble up dainties at the table, cross their legs, and tyrannize their teachers.*

—Socrates (469–399 BC)

Problems today are not new; they are just recycled and perhaps amplified by technology.

In order to continue the human species, Mother Nature endows nearly everyone with the ability to have kids. Planning for kids, however, is strictly optional. The real concern is *raising* kids.

What is the goal? Do we want to prepare kids to function in the real world? Or do we simply want them to get lost? If the challenging work of preparation is the answer, then this book will actually provide some help. Otherwise, buy some screens, and make very clear when they are supposed to move out.

When our kids were young, my wife and I were busy addressing their basic needs. There was a vague notion of where we wanted them to go, but long-term planning evolved later. We came from similar backgrounds (educational, social, economic, and religious), so our experiences, core values, and attitudes were fairly aligned. This provided at least a good starting point for parenting.

Over time, three specific elements emerged that became our top priorities. We wanted to instill them in our kids because adults who possessed these particular aspects seemed to do well in the world. The items we chose are certainly not magic bullets, but in retrospect, they worked very well for our family. Each element will be identified later in this book.

So, what do we want to give our kids? What skills do they need to succeed? Primary schools have been designed to craft a common foundation of reading, writing, mathematics, and core information. Do kids learn to memorize or to think? Do they learn to listen and speak or better yet, to debate? Can they analyze, extrapolate, apply, and create?

In her groundbreaking book *Multipliers*, Liz Wiseman identifies two types of leaders: those who build up their people and those who diminish or hold them down. The positive leaders actually multiply the output of their staff. This is accomplished not by being particularly tough and giving rigid orders but rather by asking the right questions and encouraging people to grow more than they ever imagined was possible.

Years ago, a wonderful British documentary entitled *The Seven Ups* essentially showed what time travel would be like. They recorded interviews with seven-year-old children from different socioeconomic backgrounds. The kids were observed in school and at play, and then they were asked a variety of questions. At seven-year intervals, the researchers came back to record these same children so we could observe each person as he or she evolved over a thirty-five-year period of time.

We normally see only real-time or recently recorded events. Being able to go back and forth to watch each individual growing up was unique, and the results were startling. At the age of seven, you could nearly always see how each kid would turn out as an adult. It was obvious who would become successful as well as those who would develop a dependency (drugs or alcohol). According to psychologists, by the age of seven, most of a child's hard drive has already been written.

One of our grandsons recently had his Bar Mitzvah. At thirteen, this is a challenge to young boys and girls, and it is a heck of a burden as well. But we were reminded that not too many generations ago, the age of thirteen was considered nearly half of a lifetime. Kids haven't changed, so the only difference must be our expectations of them.

This book contains lists of questions that you can ask your children, grandchildren, or even others' kids you know or meet. The questions are designed to stimulate discussions. Every answer demonstrates something, and most responses will require thoughtful explanations.

Use your judgement about how old children should be for specific questions. But keep in mind that they are almost always further along in their thinking and development than we give them credit for, so it is never too early to start.

When asked, younger children will often reflect or parrot positions that have been espoused by their parents. As they grow and assimilate more experiences and information, their positions tend to evolve. A five-year-old may answer the same question completely differently when he or she becomes ten or fifteen.

After explaining the process to those involved, the best approach is to focus on one question at a time. Actually, one per day is preferable so as not to inundate them. This also allows introspective time to process what may be new information, especially during the formative years. Simultaneously, consider how you would answer the same question.

If possible, ask several children the same question all at the same time. Allow sufficient time for them to consider their answers but be sure to set a deadline. Once everyone has given his or her response to you, ask all of them to share these same answers with the others. Then have a group discussion comparing and contrasting the answers.

We began this process during a family vacation. Our grandkids ranged in age from seven to fourteen. The question of the day was asked at breakfast, and each child had to give his or her answer to us in private before dinner. Incredibly, some of the very best answers actually came from our youngest family members.

After dinner, we had each child repeat his or her answer to the entire family so that siblings, cousins, parents, aunts, uncles, and grandparents could all hear each of the responses. This resulted in discussions that were thoughtful, funny, sensitive, sad, and sometimes even very emotional. Then we informally discussed which of the answers were among the best. Essentially, throughout this process and regardless of who gave which answer, everybody won.

Offering an incentive for good answer(s) may be necessary to initially stimulate the interaction. Over time, however, most find that the challenge to think and present one's ideas becomes self-sustaining. After a few days, the incentives were forgotten and each morning, the kids eagerly asked, "What's the question for today?"

When receiving their answer(s), it is important not to judge or negatively comment. Repeat the answer back to them in your own words to be sure you have understood their meaning. Ask questions if necessary for clarification, or have them explain or expand upon their position.

Regardless of what you may think, with questions like these, there may be lots of different responses, but keep in mind…

**There is no right or wrong answer.**

A child's limited information and perspective may be significantly different from yours. Automatically rejecting or overruling his or her answers out of hand will unfortunately eliminate your ability to have a constructive dialogue. No one likes to be told he or she is wrong. In fact, the instantaneous reaction is to become defensive and stop listening altogether.

Perhaps a better approach is to express surprise and state, "That is a very interesting answer." Ask kids to help you understand their position and have them try to convince you why you should feel the same way. By asking the right follow-up questions, it may be easier to have them understand and realize that another viewpoint might be even better.

Talking with kids in a productive dialogue is considerably different than talking at them or to them. Once you develop a routine, it will also be very interesting to ask the kids to come up with their own questions for you.

Please let us know about your own experiences and of course, any additional questions you feel should be added to our list.

Let the discussions begin!

# Questions About You

• • •

EVERYTHING STARTS WITH THE INDIVIDUAL. We began this process by simultaneously asking six grandkids the following question:

**"How do you know if someone really loves you?"**

The ages at the time ranged from seven to fourteen, and later that day, here were their answers:

- When someone tells you.
- When they do something really nice for you.
- When that person buys you gifts.
- When they want to be together and are interested in what you do and say.
- Someone who is always there for you.
- If they are your parent.

All of these were good in their own way, and we offered positive comments after each one. Then we had a group discussion about which answers were most interesting, thoughtful, innovative, and complete. Lots of emphasis was put on words versus deeds to differentiate casual and superficial from something much deeper and longer lasting. It was obvious throughout the dialogue that all of the kids were learning something, and this was the whole point.

There is one other aspect to be aware of that comes from study initially done more than fifty years ago. The approach has been replicated and proven many times since then, but sadly, few have ever heard of the Pygmalion effect.

Just before the school year started, researchers told several teachers about a test that had already been given to their incoming students. Results suggested that five particular kids would probably be the best and brightest in their class. The five students were named, and the researchers said they would return at the end of the semester in order to validate the test.

Several months later when the researchers came back, the teachers excitedly reported how successful the test was. Those students who, according to the test, were supposed to be the best and brightest turned out exactly as predicted. Then the researchers announced the surprise.

There was no test. The names of the five students were drawn randomly. The teachers were totally dumbfounded. They felt every child in the class had received the same instruction, assignments, and testing. How could five randomly identified students perform better than their peers did?

In fact, what researchers concluded was that the mere expectation of better performance was enough to influence these kids to produce at a higher level. Stated differently:

**Kids will perform up to or down to your level of expectation.**

If they know you expect them to be good or to achieve something, they will try their best to do so. Everyone will slip up from time to time, but if you continue to expect a higher standard, most of the time, it will happen.

Conversely, if you expect that they will be bad or fail at something, there is a good chance you will again be correct. And this approach works universally for parents, teachers, coaches, employers, and so on.

A corollary to this is that children who were previously recognized as disruptive but who suddenly do well in school are automatically thought to be cheating. In this situation, unfortunately, teachers are even harder on students who are behaving "out of character."

What does this say about how we view and treat our kids? More importantly, in the future, how should we craft our expectations of them?

• • •

- [ ] How do you know if someone really loves you?

- [ ] Of all the people you know or have learned about, who do you most admire, and why?

- [ ] What is your biggest problem, and how do you plan to deal with it?

- [ ] A genie offers to grant you one wish for anything in the world. What would you ask for, and why?

- [ ] When you grow up, what do you want to be, and what makes this of interest?

● ● ●

- [ ] How do you want other people to describe you?

- [ ] What is most important to you?

- [ ] How do you deal with conflict?

- [ ] Are you a leader or a follower? Give some examples.

☐ What is your favorite part of the day, and why?

• • •

☐ Describe the last thing you did for someone else. Was it out of obligation or kindness?

☐ If you could travel anywhere in the world, where would you go, and why?

☐ When should you accept a dare?

☐ Are you happy and can others around you recognize this?

☐ How can someone make you do something that you know is wrong?

• • •

☐ When is it OK to lie?

☐ Have you ever been blamed for something you did not actually do? How did it feel?

- ☐ Are you spoiled? How would others answer this question about you?

- ☐ What makes you happy?

- ☐ What makes you sad?

• • •

- ☐ If you could change one thing in your life, what would it be, and why?

- ☐ Who are you most jealous of and do you think he or she knows?

- ☐ What is the meanest thing someone has ever done to you?

- ☐ What makes you angry?

- ☐ What is the meanest thing you have ever done to someone else?

• • •

- ☐ Can you give an example of other people looking up to you?

- ☐ Why do parents say no?

- ☐ Who do you look up to, and why?

- ☐ Would you rather be with other people or be alone, and why do you feel this way?

- ☐ What are you most afraid of, and how will you get over it?

● ● ●

- ☐ What makes you cry and is it OK to do so in front of others?

- ☐ Why do you not always listen to what your parents say?

- ☐ Are you uncomfortable with anyone in particular, and what makes it so?

- ☐ How long should you know someone, and how old should you be to get married?

- ☐ What do you feel when you are late, and how do you think others feel?

● ● ●

- ☐ Why do you not always follow your parent's instructions, rules, or advice?

- ☐ What makes certain words bad?

- ☐ Which is more important: what you think about yourself or what others think about you, and why?

- ☐ Who don't you trust, and what makes you feel this way? How can that person ever regain your trust?

- ☐ How old should someone be to drink, and what should he or she be most careful of?

● ● ●

- ☐ If you found twenty dollars lying on the floor, what would you do with it?

- ☐ What are you most proud of?

- ☐ If you could do one thing all over again, what would it be?

- ☐ When you are bad, what should the punishment be?

- ☐ Who or what do you hate, and why?

● ● ●

- ☐ What is the most important lesson you have learned to date?

- ☐ What are you least proud of?

- ☐ Are you lazy? If so, is this behavior OK?

- ☐ Can you describe a situation where you felt secure or insecure?

- ☐ Which superhero would you most like to be, and why?

● ● ●

- ☐ If you could pick a different name, what would it be, and why?

- ☐ What is your favorite toy, and why?

- ☐ What would you really like to do and why?

- ☐ What is your favorite movie, and why?

- ☐ What are you really good at doing?

• • •

- ☐ What is your favorite book, and why?

- ☐ Describe a situation where you felt confident.

- ☐ Are you selfish and do others agree with this?

- ☐ What are your bad dreams about?

- ☐ When you took something that was not yours, how did it feel? Did you return it?

• • •

- ☐ What is your favorite activity, and why?

- ☐ Have you ever borrowed something but not returned it?

- ☐ How late should you be allowed to stay up at night and will this affect your ability to get up the next morning?

- ☐ Should you look in the mirror every day before leaving home, and if so, why?

- ☐ What is your least favorite activity, and what makes this so?

● ● ●

- ☐ If you could be anyone else, who would you be, and why?

- ☐ If you had to serve in the military, what capacity would you choose?

- ☐ Can you give an example of you being kind?

- ☐ What three adjectives best describe you? Explain why you choose these three.

- ☐ What is important to do when you shake hands with someone?

• • •

- ☐ When you meet new people, how can you remember their names?

- ☐ What are proper table manners?

- ☐ What is your favorite memory?

- ☐ When you don't tell the truth, how does it make you feel? Can others tell?

- ☐ Why should others trust you?

• • •

- ☐ What is your saddest memory?

- ☐ How differently does it feel when you are honest versus dishonest?

- ☐ Give an example of you being a good leader.

- ☐ Do you care what you look like to others? Why is this important or not important?

- ☐ What was your most embarrassing situation?

● ● ●

- ☐ What have you said that you later regretted? Could you take it back?

- ☐ Describe something you have done that was scary or dangerous.

- ☐ Have you ever overcome a fear? What happened, and how did it feel?

- ☐ Do you like to try new foods, and why?

- ☐ Describe a situation when you felt unsafe or in danger.

● ● ●

- ☐ Can you control yourself? Give an example of this.

- ☐ What is your biggest craving and is it good or bad for you?

- ☐ If there was no consequence, what would you binge on, and why?

- ☐ Why do people drink alcohol? When you are older, will you drink? Will you ever get drunk?

- ☐ Is smoking good or bad for people and once someone starts, is it easy to stop? What would cause you to smoke?

● ● ●

- ☐ Why do people take drugs? In the future, what would cause you to take drugs?

- ☐ Give an example of you being considerate of others.

- ☐ Is there a situation when you should talk to strangers?

- ☐ To what extent can you take care of yourself?

- ☐ What do you know how to cook, and in the future, will this be sufficient?

● ● ●

- ☐ What are the basic food groups?

- ☐ What would you do if a stranger told you to get into his or her car?

- ☐ What do you want in your obituary?

- ☐ When someone does something that is not right, do you say anything?

- ☐ Are you emotional, and how would others answer this question?

● ● ●

- ☐ Give an example of you having empathy for others.

- ☐ How do you react if you don't get your own way?

- ☐ How often do you get depressed, and can you recover on your own?

- ☐ Give an example of how you are self-motivated.

- ☐ Can you control your emotions and would others agree with you about this?

• • •

- ☐ Can you describe a situation where you play well with others?

- ☐ Are you aware of your emotions and can you feel them coming on?

- ☐ What should you do when someone gets very angry?

- ☐ Can you remember and tell funny jokes? Let's hear one.

- ☐ Describe a good trick you played on someone.

• • •

- ☐ Do you like surprises, and when was the last time one happened?

- ☐ Can you give an example of your being creative?

- ☐ Would you rather look at art or make art, and why?

☐ How does magic work?

☐ Do you want to be rich, and if so, why?

● ● ●

☐ Do you want to be famous, and if so, why?

☐ Do you have common sense and can you give an example of this.

☐ What is the difference between intelligence and common sense?

☐ Can you describe some choices that have irreversible consequences?

☐ Should people be responsible and accountable for all of their actions? Are you?

● ● ●

☐ What are you most passionate about, and why?

☐ When was the last time you were wrong about something?

- ☐ Do you know anyone who has been abused, and how do you feel about this?

- ☐ When you are old enough, will you vote, and is this really important?

- ☐ When was the last time you admitted to being wrong?

• • •

- ☐ Have you ever been abused, and how did it feel?

- ☐ What is the biggest mistake you have made? What would you do differently?

- ☐ How long do you want to live, and why?

- ☐ What do you want to accomplish in your life?

- ☐ Do you expect to be successful, and if so, how will you accomplish this?

• • •

- ☐ Do you really care what others think about you, and why?

- ☐ How can you tell when others are unhappy?

- ☐ Do you have self-esteem? Can you give an example of this?

- ☐ Would you like others to be dependent upon you, and why?

- ☐ Can you give an example of when you followed your own intuition?

● ● ●

- ☐ When was the last time you helped someone else?

- ☐ Do you appreciate what you have, and how should you show this?

- ☐ Can you give an example of where you were dependable?

- ☐ When you are frustrated, how do you deal with it?

- ☐ Is it better to ask for permission or forgiveness, and why?

● ● ●

- ☐ Have you ever backed down when you knew you were right? What happened?

- ☐ What would you change about your physical appearance? Is it all that important?

- ☐ How do you feel when you are behaving badly?

- ☐ What kind of a reputation do you have?

- ☐ Describe something that you have started.

● ● ●

# Questions About Peers

● ● ●

WE WANTED TO INSTILL IN our kids three specific characteristics. The first of these elements actually relates to interpersonal relationships. In business, society, and even in a family, social skills and awareness of others is crucial. Therefore, the first of our top priorities was…

**Self-esteem.**

How do you feel about yourself, particularly in relation to others? Are you confident and outgoing or insecure and introverted? Can you function well within a group or are you a loner? Do others perceive you to be someone they can count on, deal with, and perhaps look up to?

These qualities become even more significant as we go through life. They actually help shape both who we can become and ultimately what we can achieve. Think about anyone who is successful and you will see some of the qualities that relate to self-esteem.

Historically, IQ was felt to be a marker of future achievement; however, in the last two decades, another factor has emerged. Emotional intelligence has been shown to be even more significant in this regard. Successful people must have a certain baseline of intelligence and cognitive skill, but more important is their relative strength in five unique areas:

- Are you aware of your own emotions?
- Can you control your emotions?
- Do you have empathy for others?

- Are you self-motivated?
- Are you good in social situations?

No one actually teaches these skills, or do they? Parents can play an enormous role in helping kids to understand who they are, what they are capable of, and how to feel good about it. After all, if we do not provide this solid foundation for our offspring, who will?

● ● ●

- ☐ Who is your favorite friend, and why?

- ☐ What do friends like most about you?

- ☐ What is a "best friend forever" and should you have one?

- ☐ Does someone else consider you his or her good friend, and why?

- ☐ What do friends least like about you?

● ● ●

- ☐ What does the golden rule really mean?

- ☐ Why are some people bullies?

- ☐ How do you know if someone is not telling the truth?

- ☐ Are the most popular kids happy, and what makes you think so?

- ☐ Have you ever made fun of someone else, and how did it make you feel?

• • •

- ☐ How can you recognize a bully, and what is the best way to handle them?

- ☐ If someone revealed a secret you had shared with him or her, how would you feel?

- ☐ What is peer pressure, and how should you deal with it?

- ☐ Can bad people ever become good again; do you think this really happens?

- ☐ If a friend embarrasses or betrays you, what should you do about it?

• • •

- ☐ Have you ever called or visited a friend who was sick or injured, and how would this make him or her feel about you?

- ☐ What would make you reveal someone else's secret, and how would he or she feel if you did?

- ☐ Do you like to dance; are you any good at it?

- ☐ Is it OK to kiss and tell, and why?

- ☐ If a bully were picking on you, what would your friends do?

● ● ●

- ☐ How do you feel about Indian Guides or Scouting? What kind of clubs would you like to join, and why?

- ☐ What have you tried recently that was new, and how did it go?

- ☐ What does it mean to compromise?

- ☐ When is it OK to hit another person?

- ☐ When you meet someone new, how do you remember his or her name?

● ● ●

- ☐ If a bully were picking on your friend, what would you do?

- ☐ Can you be friends with someone of a different color? Do you have such friends?

- ☐ How do you deal with conflict?

- ☐ If you have a boy- or girlfriend, what do you like most and least about him or her?

- ☐ When someone wants to fight you, what should you do?

● ● ●

- ☐ How do you feel about other kids that are having sex? Are they open about it with others?

- ☐ Can you describe how you are a good leader?

- ☐ How are your friends similar to you?

- ☐ Since you have two ears and only one mouth, should you listen more than talk?

☐ How do you feel about kids that are taking drugs? What would you do if someone offered you drugs?

● ● ●

☐ What do you like most or least about speaking in front of a group?

☐ How are your friends different from you?

☐ How do you feel about gay people?

☐ How can you show someone that you really understood what he or she said?

☐ Should you try to control other people, and when would you want to?

● ● ●

☐ How do you feel about sex?

☐ In what ways are women and men equal and in what ways are they unequal?

- ☐ How do you feel about others having friends with benefits? Would you do this?

- ☐ Do you prefer being with one friend or being with a group, and why?

- ☐ Is it OK to have sex with multiple partners, and is this a good thing to do?

• • •

- ☐ Can other people control you, and how will you know if they are trying to?

- ☐ How would you feel about someone who is transgender?

- ☐ Can everyone really get along with each other, or is this just not possible?

- ☐ Why do people fight?

- ☐ Do you think your current friends will always be close with you, or will you make new friends over time?

• • •

☐ When two friends are fighting with each other, what should you do?

☐ Do you know anyone today that could become your partner for life? How will you know?

☐ Can you describe the kinds of discrimination that you have seen or heard about?

☐ Do you know someone who is a victim, and how do you feel toward him or her?

☐ Can you describe any discrimination that you have felt?

● ● ●

☐ Do you make decisions by yourself or base them on what others think?

☐ Are you a victim, and why do you feel this way?

☐ Do you like to go out to meet new people or stay within the circle of friends you now have?

- ☐ How does it feel to share gossip?

- ☐ What should you change to become a better friend?

• • •

- ☐ Would you like to be more popular, and if so, how will you go about it?

- ☐ When in social situations, how do you feel about drama?

- ☐ How can you avoid answering personal questions that someone asks you?

- ☐ Do others trust you, and are you worthy of their trust?

- ☐ Are you ethical? Can you give an example of this?

• • •

- ☐ Once lost, how can you regain your credibility?

- ☐ What can a person do to regain your trust?

# Family Questions

• • •

RAISING KIDS IS A UNIQUE experience that most of us learn while on the job. We observed what our parents and friends' parents did, and we may have even attempted to improve upon that approach.

Years ago, someone said, "The best way to raise kids is to have three but give away the first two." Obviously, our two oldest kids would object to this sentiment and in retrospect, so would we. The interesting point is that with more than one child, our parenting style changed over time. The eldest was subjected to a higher level of expectation and a greater pressure to achieve. This is especially true in contrast to our third child, who may have behaved exactly the same way, but by then, we were more relaxed about everything.

Case in point: With our first child, all bottles and nipples were boiled. If anything fell on the floor, it was re-sterilized or thrown away. For our second child, these same bottles and nipples were relegated to the dishwasher. The three-second rule started to be considered for anything that dropped on the floor. When our third child finally came along, basically, he shared a bowl with the dog.

Despite all of this, each of our kids has grown into a responsible adult who is now raising his or her own kids. This leads to the second priority that we wanted to give our kids.

## Independence

Translate this as developing two strong feet that children stand up on alone. What began as a parent-child bond over time evolved into an adult-adult relationship. If we do not raise our kids to be adults, who will?

By now, it should be obvious that for parents, raising kids is job number one. Very early on, a veritable contest develops between parents and babies, and this sets an underlying pattern for the future. Will they adapt to you or will you adapt to them?

A baby's needs are very basic and initially quite demanding. In spite of the perceived urgency, however, the question becomes who is the trainer and who is the trainee? Those who can appropriately interpret and endure the different patterns of crying will eventually succeed in establishing a semi controllable routine.

This is not to suggest that totally ignoring crying is acceptable since it could eventually become harmful child abuse. A distinct language of cries differentiates discomfort from actual distress. The sooner parents learn to interpret these new and sometimes-troubling sounds, the better they will be able to cope.

The unfortunate alternative is that the child learns his or her parent is totally "on call" and will eventually cave under pressure. Think about children that you have seen who have frequent meltdowns and tantrums. Either you train them or they will train you, and waiting until tomorrow to begin the process is probably not the best strategy.

In previous generations, there was less mobility, so grandparents were more proximate to young families. Their prior experience could usually provide a patient and calm demeanor to alleviate the stress of dealing with a newborn. When you are already suffering from sleep deprivation, having dependable backup is indeed a welcome relief.

An old expression suggests that there are two different ways to argue with women. Unfortunately, neither one works. Coincidently, there are many different ways to raise kids, and all of them will work, but you may not be happy with the result.

If the ultimate goal is to end up with adults, here are some insights that we have learned along the way:

1. Good parenting is clear, consistent, and always positive.
2. Parents must act in unison with a united front. Triangular relationships where a child plays one parent against the other are doomed to failure.

3. Establish house rules, boundaries, and appropriate punishments for violations. Saying "no" is important. What is done in other houses is immaterial.
4. Communicate expectations frequently—hope is not a strategy.
5. Trust and credibility are built up over time; both can be destroyed in an instant.
6. Routine chores promote individual responsibility and accountability.
7. Encourage individual decision making while considering potential risks and consequences. We sometimes learn more from our mistakes.
8. Being friendly with kids is good, but first and foremost, you must be their parent.

Each family unit is unique. As such, it is important to establish a solid foundation and structure that kids can both understand and count on as they grow and mature.

● ● ●

☐ Is your family happy, and how do you know?

☐ Should kids get an allowance or should money be earned, and why?

☐ How do you feel about everyone having chores to do at home?

☐ Someone is saying bad things about your family. What should you do about it?

☐ Why should kids have a bedtime?

● ● ●

☐ Why do parents have rules?

☐ Should your parents have more rules or fewer rules, and why?

☐ Are "sleepovers" a good practice?

☐ Which family rules are unfair?

☐ What would you like about going to camp?

• • •

☐ How do you feel about marriage?

☐ Outside of your family, who is the first person you go to with a problem, and why?

☐ How old should someone be to get married? How long should he or she think about it?

☐ What are the good things and bad things about having kids?

☐ With your own kids, what will you change from the way you were raised?

• • •

☐ What will you copy from your parents with your own kids?

☐ Are you always nice to others in your family, and why?

☐ Should families have pets, and if so, who should care for them?

☐ Are others in your family always nice to you, and why?

☐ What do you want to give to your own kids?

● ● ●

☐ How do you feel about adoption?

☐ When your own kids are bad, how will you discipline them?

☐ How does a one-parent family work?

☐ Should bad kids get spanked? Is there a better alternative?

☐ Do you know anyone who is adopted, and how do you feel about this?

● ● ●

☐ When you grow up and leave home, what will you miss the most?

☐ What was your favorite family trip?

- ☐ How do you feel about divorce?

- ☐ Are two parents necessary to raise kids?

- ☐ Is weekly family time important, and why?

● ● ●

- ☐ When one parent says no, is it OK to ask the other parent to try for a different answer? Is there a better approach?

- ☐ How would you feel if both parents are the same sex?

- ☐ Do you know anyone who has lost a family member, and how has this affected him or her?

- ☐ Do bad choices usually have consequences? Give some examples of this.

- ☐ Who suffers most in a divorce?

● ● ●

- ☐ Who will care for your parents when they get old?

- ☐ How will you feel when a member of your family dies?

- ☐ Can all consequences be changed or fixed? Can you give examples of both circumstances?

- ☐ Who would you like to care for you when you get old?

- ☐ If you were in an unhappy marriage, would you consider divorce?

● ● ●

- ☐ Do you know anyone who has been abused, and if so, could you help him or her in any way?

- ☐ What happens to kids whose parents get divorced?

- ☐ What is the difference between emotional abuse and physical abuse? Which is worse?

- ☐ What makes you believe that you will be a good parent?

- ☐ Have you ever been threatened or abused, and how did it make you feel?

● ● ●

- ☐ What is intimidation, and how should you deal with it?

- ☐ Does anyone in your family have a bad temper, and if so, how does this affect you?

- ☐ Can you describe a situation where you have been intimidated?

- ☐ Do you consider yourself dependent or independent, and why?

- ☐ When will you be an adult?

● ● ●

# Questions About Social Media

● ● ●

Every generation seems to have a unique distraction or fad. With my generation, it was the TV and pinball machines. Later on, there was the Hula-Hoop, the boom box, and tape decks. Our kids had MTV, Walkman, portable computers, and various PDAs. Next came the cell phones, iPods, iPads, and ultimately the smartphone. Do you think Steve Jobs really understood just how pervasive his creations would become?

Around the world, people are mesmerized by handheld devices. A list of what you cannot do on these magical instruments is growing shorter by the minute. Unfortunately, their usage almost seems to be narcotic. Many of the applications are not only viral but also learning exactly what you are doing so they can provide even more of it in the future.

Algorithms capture data on everything, and they determine how and when to present things back to you in order to monopolize ever more of your time. Never before have our distractions been driven by such personally focused intelligence. Is this good or bad? We probably will not know for a few more years, but there are clear signs for concern.

A high-school girl was planning to visit her older sister at college. They had exchanged e-mails and text messages planning for the weekend. One night the home phone rang, and through caller ID, the younger sister saw that it was her older sibling. Instead of answering the call, however, she simply stared at the phone in disbelief. When it kept ringing, her mother asked who was calling. The young girl said it was her sister phoning from college, and then she exclaimed in total confusion, "Why is she calling me on the telephone?"

Orphaned babies raised in very low-stimulus environments never develop the social skills to constructively interact with others. Marriages and birth rates in post-recession Europe have fallen because younger couples see diminished economics and opportunities. Countries that restricted "one child per family" now have adults that have always been the center of attention. Unusual societal systems always produce unintended consequences.

Traditional communication was thought to impact us 55 percent by body language, 38 percent by tone of voice, and only 7 percent by the words themselves. Now we are confined to abbreviated forms of typing on a screen that obscures most of the message. Handheld devices are reducing physical interaction in favor of impersonal virtual contact. Many of us have seen or heard about kids sitting next to one another and texting rather than speaking. Is this a precursor of what is yet to come?

In lieu of voice, eye contact, and touch, we are living our lives via post, tweet, or as voyeurs observing others' perfectly curated lives on their Facebook pages. Please be sure to "like me" quickly so life has real validation. Productivity is diminished by an almost uncontrollable need to check in whenever a Pavlovian sound tells us that something new has arrived.

This has totally disrupted our traditional information and business models. TV, radio, newspapers, billboards, and direct mail are all being challenged by methodologies that are newer and faster. Brick-and-mortar stores and whole shopping centers are being replaced by online malls where you can buy anything. Thus far, in the race to capture eyeballs, speed seems to be more important than personal service or accuracy.

Keeping a perspective is difficult when the world is undergoing such dramatic and rapid change. Individuals and families should find ways to balance human social interaction with screen time and virtual living. Should specific times and places be designated as "technology free" so as to maintain our humanity?

● ● ●

- ☐ What kinds of social media do you use, and how often are you on it?

- ☐ To whom do you post messages or pictures, and why?

- ☐ What are some of the apps that hide online activities and have you used them?

- ☐ Have you ever been in contact with a stranger online, and what was the outcome?

- ☐ Have you ever liked or disliked something online, and how did you feel about this?

● ● ●

- ☐ How much TV per day is OK?

- ☐ Have you ever been disliked online, and how did you feel?

- ☐ If you were not on social media, could you get work done more quickly or accurately?

- ☐ Have you ever been unfriended? What did this feel like?

☐ Have you ever been friended by someone you did not know, and did you accept him or her?

• • •

☐ How much time per day do you spend on social media, and is this too little or too much?

☐ What do you like most about social media?

☐ Can you believe everything that is online? Give an example of this.

☐ From what sources can you get factual information?

☐ Should there be a limit on screen time per day, and if so, how much is enough?

• • •

☐ Have you ever put something online that you later regretted?

☐ How do you feel about sexting with others?

- ☐ Is there a way to erase something that has been posted online or will it be around forever?

- ☐ Will online posts help or hurt when applying to a school or for a job?

- ☐ If everything put online ended up on TV, would this change what you post?

• • •

- ☐ Do you know of anyone who has been bullied on social media? Has this ever happened to you?

- ☐ When is it OK to bully someone else on social media?

- ☐ Do you know of anyone whose parents monitor their kids' online activities? Is this an invasion of privacy?

- ☐ Do you know of anyone who has suffered because of social media?

- ☐ Could you go for a full day without using the Internet? How about a week? What would it feel like to be disconnected?

• • •

- ☐ When out with other people, should you check your messages, and why?

- ☐ Have you ever texted someone who is in the same room, and is this better than talking?

- ☐ Should there be times when everyone turns off or puts away their devices, and why?

- ☐ Is it better to text or talk, and why do you feel this way?

- ☐ When communicating, which is most important: words, tone, or body language?

● ● ●

- ☐ How effective is electronic communication that can only convey words?

- ☐ What are your favorite apps, and why do you like them? How often do your favorites change?

- ☐ Do you enjoy online games, and are you any good at them?

- ☐ Would you rather play online games with friends or strangers, and why?

- ☐ What do you learn from social media?

● ● ●

- ☐ Are you on Facebook, and is this important to you?

- ☐ What don't your parents know about social media that they should?

- ☐ Why do you look at other people's Facebook pages?

- ☐ Does anyone ever post things that are unflattering about themselves, or does everything online seem to be perfect?

- ☐ Are people's lives really as good as they appear online?

● ● ●

- ☐ Is it better to spend time doing virtual things or doing real things?

# Questions About Education

• • •

We give kids lots of stuff throughout their lives. When new, it may be exciting and hold their interest for a while. Over time, however, things wear out and become less shiny, and they are eventually relegated to a corner or closet. For some, the very acquisition of material goods becomes an all-consuming way of life. Is the person with the most stuff the happiest?

The third major element that we wanted to provide for our kids was something that would never get old, tarnish, or go out of style. Therefore, our final priority was to provide a quality…

**Education.**

Memorizing facts and figures is important, but our interest was more in developing

- Critical thinking,
- Analytical reasoning,
- Innovative and creative skills, and
- Communication skills.

If natural curiosity and questioning is encouraged, the result will be lifelong learning. This makes education an ongoing dynamic rather than a static period of spoon feeding answers to test questions.

We were products of public school and wanted our kids to have similar experiences. Unfortunately, in our area, the neighborhood schools were quite inconsistent. Some teachers were highly motivated and very involved with their students while others seemed to be impatiently waiting for retirement. Our professions (construction and makeup) did not offer tenure, so this employment concept popularized by academia was foreign to us.

For the most part, public schools are structured after the old British educational model. When England was a world power, the country needed competent clerks and managers who could read, write, and do basic mathematics. They designed an age-based batch process model with teachers instructing students in each of these subjects. Grading was used to identify those who could successfully achieve the required skills.

In spite of advances in technology and the increased ability of kids to process information more rapidly, many schools continue using this same old approach. Is it any wonder that some students get bored and completely turned off by an antiquated model?

Some well-intentioned school boards and teacher groups seemed more concerned about maintaining their control and the status quo rather than updating the process and truly educating their students.

In 1960, many high schools had vocational programs to teach manual skills to non-college-bound kids. Students could try a variety of professions, which ultimately led to productive careers in many areas. For some reason, educators subsequently decided that everyone should go to college, and most of these vocational programs were eliminated. The unintended consequence is that a majority of the supposedly "college-prepared" students never graduated from an accredited university. To further compound the problem, they now were totally unprepared for any type of career.

At its peak, America used to employ twenty-one million people in manufacturing. According to one recent report, we now have just twelve million people actually making things. This is not to say that nine million jobs have gone offshore. To the contrary, manufacturing today is so efficient that we are making even more stuff now, with considerably fewer people.

After President Bill Clinton signed the School-to-Work Opportunities Act in 1994, we created a Houston-area Construction Industry Coalition to put it in place. This act encouraged schools to partner with apprenticeship programs to replicate the vocational model from the past. Our group offered free training for all kids and guaranteed summer internships in every facet of construction.

Twelve months later, after visiting virtually every school district in the region, we ended up getting absolutely no kids. Do you know what the last seven words of a dying business model are? "But we've always done it that way!" Please turn off the lights when you go.

Governmental and educational bureaucracies do not know what jobs to train people for. Existing industries are being dislocated at an ever-accelerating rate. Does anyone doubt that driverless vehicles will eventually be commonplace? Whether this happens in five or ten years does not really matter. When it occurs, what happens to the millions of people who currently earn their living by driving, repairing, or insuring vehicles?

There are signs that vocational programs are making a comeback, and this is very timely. Schools should teach kids basic information and cognitive skills that can be used in any career. They should also partner with local and regional companies to develop apprenticeship programs that lead to real jobs that are or will be in demand.

High-school guidance counselors in Germany and Japan are charged with helping each child find a career path. That may be a college program or it could be some industry-specific training that leads to a real job. Educational and vocational testing also helps individuals decide what direction to pursue. Why not adopt this as our model?

Despite the cost, our family decided to investigate private schools, and we found in general, they offered much more rigorous and challenging programs. Our kids were well prepared for college, and with one exception, they graduated and individually pursued advanced education as well.

The one exception is well worth further explanation. We told each of our kids that we would pay for whatever college they got into subject, however, to several conditions. This was how we crafted our expectations.

- They had four years to graduate.
- They had to maintain an average of B's or better.
- At the end of college, they had to have a job or career path.

Our daughter chose to pursue a degree in communications with a goal of becoming a sports broadcaster. We questioned the practicality of this decision but did not stand in the way. Toward the end of her first semester, she called and asked to renegotiate our deal. Apparently, the program was not going to lead to her goal, and she decided to become a nurse instead.

When asked what made her think at this point that she could even get into a nursing program, she totally surprised us. A quality nursing school at another college had already accepted her. While being proud of her initiative and veracity, we asked what had to be altered. Not all of her first year credits could be transferred to nursing, so she wanted us to restart the four-year clock.

What would you have done? After a brief discussion, we agreed to her request. Four years later, our daughter graduated with honors, went right to work, and never looked back. Subsequently, she even returned to school all on her own to get an MBA. Now she has a profession that is well rewarded, totally portable, and necessary everywhere in the world. This is why to us education is so vitally important.

● ● ●

☐ Why go to school?

☐ What do you most want to get from attending school?

☐ Who is your favorite teacher, and why?

☐ Why are some kids disruptive in class?

☐ What is your best subject, and why?

● ● ●

☐ What do you most like about school?

☐ What is your worst subject, and why?

☐ What kinds of things do you like to read?

☐ What do you want the school yearbook to say about you?

☐ Do you think you are smart compared to others?

● ● ●

☐ Does homework really matter?

☐ What makes a good teacher?

☐ Do you consider yourself to be a good teacher, and why?

☐ How do you learn best: reading, listening, watching, or doing? Give an example of this.

☐ What is your favorite book, and why?

● ● ●

☐ Do you want your parents to check on your homework, and why?

☐ Why are grades important?

☐ Do you introduce yourself to new classmates or wait for them to approach you first?

☐ What was the most important lesson that you have ever learned?

☐ Should kids attend school all year?

● ● ●

☐ Is it necessary to get all As, and why?

☐ Is grading on a curve fair to everyone or does it hurt those who are best prepared?

☐ Give an example of something you have taught to another person. How did this make you feel?

☐ How will school help you in the future?

☐ Should teachers be able to discipline bad students, and if so, what should be allowed?

● ● ●

☐ How much school do you need?

☐ How are computers helping kids to learn?

- ☐ Do you ever have a question but decide not to ask it? What causes this to happen?

- ☐ When should someone be kicked out of school, and should they be allowed to return?

- ☐ Is it more important to know or to think, and why?

● ● ●

- ☐ Should everyone go to college? What should happen to kids that are not going to college?

- ☐ Why are standardized tests important?

- ☐ Is there any benefit to learning a foreign language? Should this be required?

- ☐ Should teachers present basic information or teach test questions, and why?

- ☐ What classes would you want added to your school?

● ● ●

- ☐ How should you go about selecting a college?

- ☐ Are trade schools and apprenticeship programs important? Who should attend them?

- ☐ Is it important to learn about music and art, and why?

- ☐ What kind of student do you want your kids to be?

- ☐ Should schools have competitive sports teams, and why?

● ● ●

- ☐ Should everyone get a free education through college and beyond? Would this be good or bad?

- ☐ When should teachers get fired?

- ☐ What is the difference between public versus private schools, and which are better?

- ☐ What did you not learn in school that you should have?

☐ Should families have a choice of which school to put their children into, and would you have chosen a different school?

• • •

☐ Are charter schools or voucher programs good or bad for students and in what ways?

☐ How will you find a good career?

☐ Should the smart kids be in different classes, and why?

☐ Should kids who have learning challenges be mainstreamed or placed in specialized classes, and why?

☐ What kind of school will you send your kids to, and what is your goal for them?

• • •

# Questions About Beliefs

• • •

WHEN OUR KIDS WERE VERY young, they began questioning where babies came from. Their grandmother was apparently not satisfied with our simplistic and age-appropriate answers. She took it upon herself to find and send us a book with pictures that would better explain the entire process to them. When it arrived, we dutifully read the book with our kids, knowing that Nanny would be conducting her usual follow up.

She got on the phone with our son and asked, "Did you read the book?" He proudly said, "Yes, Nanny, we finished it last night." Her next question was "So, tell me where you come from." Somewhat perplexed, he said, "Nanny, I come from St. Louis. Don't you already know that?"

The concepts of God and religion probably evolved when humankind had more questions than answers. What better way to explain things perceived as well above our paygrade. Religion gave us a reason, a code for living, and a moral compass to act as an anchor.

While life on earth may not have been a blessing, as long as we followed the rules, there was the promise of heaven. The rules were meant to differentiate right from wrong, good from evil, and God from the devil. In a constructive society, people needed some definitions of what was considered acceptable behavior. Whether they were golden rules like "do unto others," a list of ten items on stone tablets, or books filled with historical narratives and vague parables, all were designed to form a cultural foundation.

Exclusivity was important. Followers must know their way was correct and that others were descending rather than ascending. Depending upon the veracity or aggressiveness of the group, outsiders could be converted, enslaved, or sent to find out if their own God was real. Over the centuries, some religions have disappeared, some have evolved, and a few have rigidly maintained their ancient traditions.

In the modern world, we have plenty of answers but may have lost our curiosity to keep asking questions. Membership numbers and attendance at services for many faiths is in decline. Does religion play a significant role in your life? Will succeeding generations feel the same way?

● ● ●

- ☐ Do you believe in God? Why?

- ☐ Does prayer work and can you give an example?

- ☐ Why is there religion in the world?

- ☐ Is heaven a real place, and if so, what is it like?

- ☐ How often do you pray, and is this enough?

● ● ●

- ☐ Does God control everything? If not, what doesn't he control?

- ☐ What happens to atheists?

- ☐ Why is honor important?

- ☐ Do you think people are good because if not, God will punish them?

- ☐ Who goes to heaven, and why?

● ● ●

☐ What are your most important core values?

☐ How do you think religion started?

☐ What are the Ten Commandments?

☐ Do you believe in original sin, and how does this affect the way you live?

☐ Why are there so many different religions?

● ● ●

☐ Should people forgive, and why do you feel this way?

☐ Is religion important to you, and why?

☐ Are people who practice religions other than ours wrong or bad, and why?

☐ Does God forgive? Can you give an example of this?

☐ Do animals go to heaven? What about bad animals?

• • •

☐ Does charity work, and how do you know?

☐ Do you believe in reincarnation, and how would this work?

☐ Is it more important to donate money or time? Which would feel better?

☐ Why do some people give anonymously?

☐ Why do bad things sometimes happen to good people?

• • •

☐ Have you ever donated or given anything to charity, and how did it feel?

☐ Can you be friends with someone of a different religion, and how do you know this?

☐ Have you ever had to accept charity, and how do you think the people who donated felt about this?

☐ When parents come from two different religions, what religion are the kids?

☐ What makes someone spiritual?

• • •

☐ Why do some people who claim to be religious act in a contrary manner?

☐ Can sinners really repent? Do people really change or just say they will?

☐ How is our religion different from others?

☐ Do you think all spiritual leaders practice what they preach, and does God know if they do?

☐ What do most religions have in common?

• • •

☐ Why do some religions fight with others?

☐ What is a martyr, and why would someone choose to become one?

☐ How often should people go to services, and is this important?

☐ Can religion solve everything or are somethings left up to people?

☐ Are some religions excessive or oppressive, and who is to judge this?

● ● ●

☐ Are all religions protected in America or only the good ones?

☐ Should everyone get to choose their own religion, and why?

☐ Do you believe in abortion or is this always a bad thing?

☐ What does it mean to turn the other cheek?

- ☐ Should abortion be decided by an individual or the government?

• • •

- ☐ What religions do your friends practice? Have you ever observed or experienced their religion?

- ☐ Can anyone really prove that God exists, or is this just something people choose to believe?

- ☐ Must a person attend formal services to be religious or is there another way?

- ☐ Should the strong dominate the weak, and why?

- ☐ How can someone who does not practice religion still be spiritual?

• • •

- ☐ How can those who believe "thou shall not kill" fight wars?

- ☐ Is it OK to ask questions about your religion or faith, and have you ever done so?

- ☐ Do you believe in free will or fate, and why?

- ☐ Did God create humans, or did they evolve through nature? Can we prove this?

- ☐ Why do some religions treat men and women differently? Is this good or bad, and why?

• • •

- ☐ Is it more important to follow religious rules or government laws, and why?

- ☐ Should our country allow Muslim women to cover their faces, and how would you feel if you were required to be covered?

- ☐ Do you believe men and women are equal, and why?

- ☐ Should we take the Bible literally, figuratively, or some other way?

- ☐ Does Sharia law conflict with US law, and if so, in what ways?

• • •

- ☐ What is the difference between the Old Testament and the New Testament?

- ☐ Should we allow people to worship the devil or someone other than God?

- ☐ Is there a respectful way to destroy an old Bible or Koran (Qur'an), and if so, how should it be done?

- ☐ What are atheists, and how do they practice?

- ☐ Why did so many religions start in the Middle East?

● ● ●

- ☐ Does God speak to individuals, and is there any proof of this?

- ☐ Who wrote the Bible and when was it written?

- ☐ Are you spiritual, and how would others know of this?

# Questions About Authority

• • •

*I fight authority, authority always wins.*

—John Cougar Mellencamp

The world is filled with figures of authority and the myriad of rules they promulgate. This occurs in peer groups, families, on social media, schools, religious institutions, sports, business, and of course government. Everywhere we turn, someone is always in charge, and he or she is ready, willing, and able to tell us exactly how to do things.

Authority is here to stay. As such, the real question becomes how we react to it. Should we be compliant or combative? Does this depend more on our personality or on our experience and perspective? One of the pillars of American society is the rule of law. This applies equally to all citizens, or does it?

Those raised in a secure environment may have developed a trust and respect for law enforcement. How about those growing up where crime is rampant, murders are frequent, and drugs are plentiful? Do people from Ferguson, Missouri, or the South Side of Chicago feel the same way about police as those living in areas that are more affluent?

Trust and respect cannot be legislated or demanded. Both must be earned, and if ever betrayed, they evaporate in a heartbeat. Our attitude toward authority is formed over time by our family and our environment. Once this has been established, we tend to read, listen more to, and believe that which reinforces our acquired viewpoint.

We are also predisposed by nature with certain built-in reflexes. A plastic owl on the roof will scare other birds away even if they have never seen a live owl. Psychologists have shown disturbing images to people so quickly that the brain cannot understand exactly what the picture showed. Despite this fact, the body instantaneously demonstrates increased levels of stress. We may be intelligent, logical, and completely without prejudice, but overcoming our hard drive is practically impossible.

The best we can do is to understand that everyone has predispositions and a unique hard drive. Those in authority generally have the upper hand. When we perceive that certain actions have become unreasonable or crossed a line, the natural reaction is to challenge. The amygdala may automatically compel us toward fight or flight. Immediately reacting to authority is rarely necessary or very productive.

Several years ago, the American Bar Association ran a program with inner-city schoolchildren. The goal was to teach alternative dispute resolution. Normally, kids who feel threatened react almost immediately with fists or other weapons. This was the primary way to stand up and defend friends, position, or honor.

The lawyers acknowledged this practice and engaged the class to identify each of the potential consequences. Most schools automatically expel students for fighting, and of course, significant injury to someone else could result in jail time. Many kids already knew people in jail, so this was not a clear deterrence.

Was there a way, the lawyers asked, to stand up for yourself and not get kicked out of school or thrown in jail? After much discussion, they taught kids how to deal with anger and essentially gain control of their emotions. Following the program, teachers in classes and on playgrounds observed the results. Angry kids were still balling up their fists but hesitating to evaluate their options. In most cases, they ended up hurling words rather than punches.

Hopefully, emotional intelligence will allow us to stop, analyze consequences, and choose the best course of action. Everyone must learn to constructively deal with people in charge. The all-pervasive smartphones have become the worst nightmare for overly aggressive authoritarians. There is an optimal time and place to challenge authority, and rarely is it right now.

● ● ●

- [ ] Who do you most trust, and why?

- [ ] Should you respect parents, and do you always show respect for yours?

- [ ] Do you trust police officers, and why?

- [ ] Do you respect your teacher(s), and how does this evolve?

- [ ] Is your principal fair, and can you give an example of this?

● ● ●

- [ ] Who is more important: a police officer, a politician, or a religious leader, and why?

- [ ] Do you believe in the death penalty? Why do you feel this way?

- [ ] Should doing drugs be illegal or should people be left to do whatever they want?

- [ ] Should getting drunk be a crime or is this an individual choice?

☐ How many different law enforcement agencies exist in our area?

• • •

☐ If a police officer is chasing you, what should you do?

☐ Should everyone be considered innocent until proven guilty? Does this always happen?

☐ Should criminals who commit multiple crimes serve longer sentences? Does this actually deter crime?

☐ Should marijuana users go to jail or is this a victimless crime?

☐ Should marijuana dealers be sent to jail or should this be a minor infraction?

• • •

☐ Are all police shootings justified? How do you know?

☐ If your car is stopped by a police officer, what should you do?

- ☐ Should people own guns or should they all be illegal, and why?

- ☐ Must all guns and gun owners be licensed, and does this affect crime?

- ☐ How do we make schools safer?

• • •

- ☐ Do you feel safe in your home? What would make you feel safer?

- ☐ Is your neighborhood safe, and why?

- ☐ When should you run away from a police officer?

- ☐ What makes you feel unsafe?

- ☐ Do you know how to safely handle guns or would you like to learn, and why?

• • •

# Questions About Sports

● ● ●

Unless you are a total recluse, life itself is a team sport. We constantly interact with others. At work, there are innumerable offices, departments, divisions, and other corporate structures. We serve in various positions on working groups, committees, and boards. Similar configurations are found in schools, trade groups, religious facilities, and even volunteer organizations.

Working with others is required at home as well. Everyone is assigned a position that has its own roles and responsibilities. Just like in sports, people learn to cover for one another and become aware of their strengths and weaknesses. The underlying concept of teamwork forms the basis for most interpersonal activities.

Why are sports so important? When playing on a team, we learn such things as discipline, focus, rules, statistics, scoring, losing, and winning. Structured competition teaches us to work together and provides a healthy outlet. Physical activity also helps to develop hand-eye coordination, stimulate the brain, generate endorphins, and relieve stress and anxiety. Without question, healthy bodies contribute to healthy minds.

The book *Younger Next Year* by coauthors Dr. Henry Lodge and his patient, Chris Crowley, explores how aggressive physical activity helps the body continue to think it is young. In order to survive, cave dwellers had to run very fast to catch sufficient protein. This stimulates production of a natural drug that tells the body to rebuild itself so that tomorrow, more protein can be caught. They advocate good diet, moderate alcohol, and aggressive physical activity to keep the body rebuilding.

Some very good lessons are learned in competition. How do you match up against a competitor? Who wants it more and therefore is better prepared? Both winning and losing are huge experiences that can help people grow. If as people say you learn from your mistakes, then we are almost experts.

One of our granddaughters was bragging about being a professional. We had recently watched her perform at a very fancy ballet recital, and the following day, she competed well in softball. Achieving this professional designation, however, was totally confusing to us. When asked, "In what activity was she considered a professional?"

The answer made us all laugh. This eight-year-old (going on twenty) child claimed to be a ***professional non listener.*** At least now, we know why she has difficulty following parental instructions.

● ● ●

- ☐ Do you enjoy sports, and if so, which ones?

- ☐ Are you a good athlete and can you give an example of this?

- ☐ Are you a good sport? What would others say about you?

- ☐ Is being a good athlete important, and why?

- ☐ How do you get better at a sport?

• • •

- ☐ Do other people want you on their team? How does this make you feel?

- ☐ Who was your favorite coach, and what made him or her so?

- ☐ Are you fair? Give some examples.

- ☐ Have you learned anything from playing sports? What do you hope to learn?

- [ ] How does it make you feel when you see a poor loser?

● ● ●

- [ ] Are you a poor loser, and can there be a good loser?

- [ ] Do you like competition? What are some examples of this?

- [ ] Should there be trophies for participation or just for winning, and why?

- [ ] Do you prefer individual sports or team activities, and why?

- [ ] How do you feel when listening to others brag about their achievements?

● ● ●

- [ ] Can a team win every time? What is a more realistic expectation?

- [ ] Do you ever brag about your performances, and how does this make you feel?

- ☐ How can you console a teammate who makes a mistake?

- ☐ Have you ever complimented someone who did well, and how do you think he or she felt?

- ☐ During a game, can you see when other people make mistakes? Can you see your own mistakes as well? How could this help?

• • •

- ☐ Are some people natural athletes? Can you give any examples?

- ☐ Are you jealous of players who are better or are you happy for them? Do they know how you feel?

- ☐ Do you want to be a professional athlete, and why?

- ☐ Do you think becoming a professional athlete is a realistic goal for someone, and why?

- ☐ Would you be a better player or coach, and what makes you think so?

• • •

- ☐ Which is more important for a good athlete: attitude or experience? Why?

- ☐ What is hand-eye coordination, and can it be learned?

- ☐ Can you name any professional athletes who did not make their high-school teams? Do you think this was their fault or the coach's fault?

- ☐ When should players be cocky? How does this make you feel?

- ☐ How do you feel about cheaters, and what should you do about them?

● ● ●

- ☐ What is overconfidence, and have you ever experienced this?

- ☐ Is "how you play the game" really important? Why?

- ☐ Does learning teamwork help you later in life? Give an example.

- ☐ What are your favorite sports, and why?

- Who are your sports heroes, and what makes them so?

• • •

- Would you rather watch a game or play a game, and why?

- Do you ever gamble on sports? Should players be allowed to gamble, and why?

- In baseball, what is considered a good batting average, and why is it not even higher?

- How do you get faster?

- Why is endurance important, and how do you achieve it?

• • •

- How is being physically fit good for your health?

- What makes a team good?

- What kind of coach do you like?

- ☐ Are player and game statistics important, and if so, why?

- ☐ Would you rather read about sports or watch a game? Why?

● ● ●

- ☐ If a player is already good, why does he or she have to practice?

- ☐ What makes a good coach?

- ☐ Is team discipline important? Who is responsible for maintaining discipline?

- ☐ Do you have to like every member of your team? Do you have to respect them and why?

- ☐ When you lose, how does it feel to congratulate the winner?

● ● ●

- ☐ What makes good sportsmanship?

# Questions About Money

• • •

*For the love of money is the root of all evil: which while some coveted after, they have erred from the faith, and pierced themselves through with many sorrows.*

—Timothy 6:10

This biblical quote suggests that money is inherently bad. Historically, the church forbade its members from charging interest on loans, but this restriction has long since been eliminated. The currency itself has no particular qualities. Individuals are the ones who determine whether money is put to good or bad use.

We wanted our kids to understand and appreciate the value of money. For personal spending, rather than allowances, our kids had to find jobs. At fifteen, each child in turn applied for a sacker position at the neighborhood grocery store. After interviews, Mr. Adams, the store manager, hired our first two kids as sackers, and they made minimum wage.

The "big" money came from customer tips. Most people appreciated the kids who carried grocery bags out to the car. Workers who figured this out could identify which customers were most likely to be generous. Surprisingly, some well-known figures such as professional athletes rarely tipped. More research would be required to understand if this was a personal or cultural trait.

By the time our third child applied for a job, the store had implemented a "truth test" for all job applicants. The grocery industry's profit margin is so slim that it wants to avoid hiring anyone who might further reduce the bottom line. One of the early test questions was "What is the total value of merchandise that you and your friends have shoplifted?"

After answering zero dollars to this question, our son casually looked at the other applicants who were taking the same test. They all appeared to be mentally calculating an approximate value. Guess who got a job offer? Instead of a sacker, he was hired as a checker to ring the register and handle cash. A fifteen-year-old who did not get an allowance was disappointed by being given a slightly higher salary because there would be no tips.

People are generally either spenders or savers. The former are always buying new and better stuff while the latter are more frugal and save for a rainy day. When you are young, there is plenty of time to save for retirement. Time, however, accelerates as you age. Before you realize, it is almost too late to put aside enough to live on.

It is never too early to learn about money. Everyone should understand about bank accounts, credit cards, financing major purchases, and paying interest. When making a salary, how much do you end up with and where do all of the deductions go? Taxes may not be important to anyone until he or she begins working. This is when lessons in finance become really important.

● ● ●

- ☐ Where does money come from?

- ☐ Why do people work?

- ☐ Which is better: cash or credit? Why?

- ☐ Can you explain if you are a spender or a saver?

- ☐ How does someone become successful?

● ● ●

- ☐ Is it better to spend or save, and why?

- ☐ Is money important, and could you live with less?

- ☐ Is it better to be smart or rich, and why?

- ☐ How does a checkbook work?

☐ How do debit cards differ from credit cards, and why are both available?

• • •

☐ What does it mean to be rich?

☐ When should you borrow money, and whom could you get it from?

☐ Should you have your own bank account, and if so, what is required?

☐ What is the difference between a checkbook and savings account? Can you balance a checkbook?

☐ Do you want to be rich, and if so, why?

• • •

☐ What is interest, who sets the rate, and how does it get paid?

☐ What are minimum payments, and is there any consequence in making them?

- ☐ What happens if you cannot pay your bills?

- ☐ What would you do to become rich? What would you not do?

- ☐ How old must you be to get a credit card, and what happens if someone else gets your information?

• • •

- ☐ What is a credit score, and how does it work?

- ☐ Why would someone have multiple credit cards?

- ☐ Is it important to completely pay off credit cards? Why?

- ☐ Is there a difference between banks and credit unions? What are both used for?

- ☐ How do you get a loan, and what will a lender look at before giving you money?

• • •

- [ ] How do you buy a car or house?

- [ ] What is a mortgage, and how does it work?

- [ ] How much do your phone and computer cost per month? What added charges could there be?

- [ ] How much does it cost to operate a car each year, and what is included in this amount?

- [ ] How much does it cost to operate a house each year, and what is included in this amount?

● ● ●

- [ ] How much does it cost to operate a boat each year, and what is included in this amount?

- [ ] What does a vacation cost, and what is included in this amount?

- [ ] How much does school cost per year, and what is included in this amount?

- [ ] What is sales tax, how is it calculated, and who pays it?

☐ What is income tax, how is it calculated, and who pays it?

• • •

☐ How many different doctors do you see a year, and what is the cost?

☐ Should you have health insurance, what would it cost, what would it cover, and what would you still have to pay for?

☐ How much do meals cost, including tax and tip, and how are these extras figured?

☐ Should people have life insurance? What are the different types, what is the cost, and which is better?

☐ How much money will you spend this year, and will the amount change over time?

• • •

☐ What would it cost for you to live on your own, and how could you afford to do this?

☐ What is welfare, who gets it, and how does it work?

- ☐ What does it cost per year to raise a family, and what is included in this amount?

- ☐ Why does the government help some people, and should this be subject to any conditions or requirements?

- ☐ Is it better to have someone else take care of you or to live on your own, and why?

• • •

- ☐ When you retire, how much money will you need to live on, and where will it come from?

- ☐ When you are working for twenty-five dollars per hour, will you receive all of this money, and if not, what gets deducted, and why?

- ☐ How much tax is fair?

- ☐ Name at least five different ways to get money.

- ☐ Do you like to gamble, and in what game are the odds in your favor?

• • •

- ☐ As you make more money, should tax rates stay the same or go higher, and why?

- ☐ Would you loan money to a friend, and if so, what would your terms be?

- ☐ Is playing the lottery a good bet, and what are the chances of winning?

- ☐ If you loaned someone money and he or she didn't pay it back, what recourse is there?

- ☐ Would you borrow money from family or friends, and why?

• • •

- ☐ How much money is "enough"?

- ☐ If you were as rich as Bill Gates, how would you use your wealth?

- ☐ What is a will, and how does it work?

- ☐ At death, will you pass wealth on to your family or donate it to charity, and why?

# Questions About Government

• • •

FOLLOWING WORLD WAR II, AMERICA was in full stride. We could do almost anything. Business was flourishing, jobs were abundant, and most people were hopeful for a better future.

Since then, government has grown significantly and taken on many more roles and responsibilities. This is the very nature of power and control. Individuals and organizations that have power will do everything they can to maintain and even expand their reach and authority. Some would say that a strong government leads to a strong country. Others argue that as government has become more controlling and overly intrusive, it has in fact become an impediment to economic growth.

Americans have become so polarized that our consensus form of government no longer appears to work. There is plenty of shouting and hyperbolic exaggeration. But the focus is more on attacking people rather than problems. Bad news and fear are great motivators, especially in elections. All it takes is fake news or the proper "spin" to smear an opponent.

In the absence of term limits, many elected officials keep their positions for long periods. Incumbents have a huge advantage over challengers. Instead of being covered by Social Security, government workers today receive pension plans substantially more generous than in the private sector. We vote for people because they have all of the answers, but once in office, very little gets done.

The higher an elected office, the more money is needed to maintain one's position. Fund raising is a never-ending task. There is no better way to do this than the Chicken Little approach: keep telling constituents "The sky is falling."

Both parties have rigidly staked out their positions. Today they would rather sit on their hands than compromise and allow the opposition even a pyrrhic victory. The big rocks are all still there. Some have even become sacred and untouchable despite the fact that they block our path forward and in their present form are not sustainable.

The world and to a certain extent our country still has war, hunger, disease, and poverty. These things continue unabated despite the advances made in other areas. While America used to represent progress and opportunity, many have lost their sense of optimism and perhaps our very way.

We have seen many wonderful things from science, medicine, and technology. The quality of life has significantly improved, but these benefits have not been uniformly experienced in our society. Glaring disparity continues to exist, and the gap between the haves and have nots seems to be widening. American infrastructure that used to be second to none is now falling behind much of the rest of the developed world.

Do you trust government? A joint biography titled *The Brothers: John Foster Dulles, Allen Dulles, and Their Secret World War* by Stephen Kinzer may provide a surprising viewpoint. During the 1950s, these former corporate lawyers simultaneously served as the secretary of state and director of the CIA. Clients who had problems with any foreign leader could count on the Dulles brothers to remedy the situation.

Most times the foreign leader was declared a Communist, and the United States would step in and replace him with someone more amenable. When the government of Premier Mohammed Mosaddeq started interfering with Western oil interests in 1953, we helped to overthrow him. The pro-West shah of Iran was placed into power, and now you know why the leaders of that country hate us. In 1954, the United Fruit Company was similarly assisted in Guatemala to maintain its banana monopoly.

In Vietnam, Ho Chi Minh and his people fought the French for years. Twice he wrote President Harry Truman asking for help to gain the country's independence as we had against the British. The French were our allies, so interfering was not an option. Once the French lost and left the country, however, the United States could have reached out and helped him develop the country.

Despite French warnings, the Dulles brothers decided they could easily topple this peasant, and thus began our involvement in Southeast Asia.

The 1961 Bay of Pigs disaster in Cuba marked the end of the Dulleses' foreign-policy era. Were Communism and the cold war really behind every threat, or were they just veils used to conceal our own involvement?

The banking industry is largely blamed for the housing crisis that resulted in the 2008 recession. During both the Clinton and Bush administrations, the government actually coerced banks to increase mortgage lending to lower-income applicants. Homeowners care for property better than renters, and this would stabilize neighborhoods. Kids that did not have to move every six months (for lower rent) would also do better in school.

Regardless of who originated these home loans, Fannie Mae and Freddie Mac agreed to underwrite them. These semi government agencies paid huge bonuses to their leaders based on the volume of mortgages that were being written. They also made campaign contributions, employed friends and relatives of politicians, and opened branch offices in many Republican and Democratic districts.

Everyone had a vested interest in continuing the housing boom. In retrospect, lowering qualification standards to achieve greater home ownership was a huge mistake. As a result, America and much of the world suffered.

Given all of our progress, we still have too many people who are unable to achieve their full potential. Poverty and under employment remain ongoing problems. More than fifty years have been spent trying to solve racial issues. But has there been any significant improvement? We continue doing the same things over and over again, apparently in the hope that the outcome will be different. Sadly, this is the definition of insanity.

Our tax laws are so complex that few people are able to prepare their own tax returns. In Vietnam, private citizens can file their returns online in less than five minutes. According to MSNBC, American companies currently have about $2.5 trillion in cash held overseas. This money was earned in and taxed by foreign countries. If this cash is brought home now, the IRS will charge 35 percent tax on top of what has already been paid. Would it be bad if all of this money were in our banks instead of foreign banks?

The Department of Interior posts signs at all national parks asking people not to feed the animals because they will become dependent. At the same time, the Department of Health was celebrating that over forty million people were now receiving some type of food assistance. Its goal was to find ways to provide even more. Does ongoing government assistance eventually make people independent or actually conspire to keep them dependent? Clearly, we want to help those in need. But what is the goal?

According to our Declaration of Independence, "All men are created equal." Today, however, we have defined many different types of "victims." Is every victim status a label for life? Does each type require its own unique set of laws? Does this approach change individual behaviors and attitudes or merely serve as grounds for lawsuits?

Should government try to do more or should it focus on the things it can do well? Should certain functions be outsourced to the private sector? The answer may depend upon perspective. Are you on the giving end or the receiving end? If less than half of all Americans currently pay federal income tax, this point may be moot.

We may have the best government money can buy, but the real question is, can we afford it?

• • •

☐ What do you most like and dislike about our country?

☐ What is a democracy, and how does it work?

☐ Who has the right to vote, and who is not allowed to exercise this right?

☐ What basic freedoms do we enjoy?

☐ What kind of action or behavior is appropriate when the national anthem is played?

● ● ●

☐ What percentage of people actually votes, and what does this suggest?

☐ What are the three main branches of government, and why do they exist?

☐ How do you feel about patriotism?

☐ Do you trust the government? Why?

- ☐ Some countries have a class system. What is this and do we have it in our country?

• • •

- ☐ What are the checks and balances in our government, and do they work?

- ☐ What things should government do?

- ☐ What is the rule of law, and do you believe it works for everyone?

- ☐ What things should government not do?

- ☐ Do we need more laws or do we have too many already? Why do you think that?

• • •

- ☐ Should everyone be required to serve their country, and if so, in what capacity?

- ☐ Name three things government does well and explain why.

- ☐ In the last presidential election, whom would you have voted for, and why?

- ☐ Do you trust politicians, and why do you feel this way?

- ☐ What are the differences between Republicans and Democrats?

• • •

- ☐ Are you a Republican, a Democrat, or something else, and why?

- ☐ Is our form of government working, and is there a way to make it better?

- ☐ Should people be allowed to speak negatively about our country, and how should this be controlled?

- ☐ Under what circumstances would you fight for our country?

- ☐ What are the best ways to question or challenge government policies and actions?

• • •

- ☐ What are lobbyists and special interests, and do we need them?

- ☐ When is it OK to burn the American flag, and why?

- ☐ How does the Electoral College work and do we still need it?

- ☐ Who decides how big the government should be, and who pays for it?

- ☐ What are the pros and cons of government workers belonging to unions?

● ● ●

- ☐ What percentage of our income should be used to operate the government?

- ☐ What are immigrants, and how do they get here?

- ☐ How does someone become a US citizen?

- ☐ Who writes laws, how many are there, and does anyone know all of them?

- ☐ Must all laws be obeyed? Why?

● ● ●

- ☐ Who enforces laws, and what happens if you break a law but no one sees it?

- ☐ Can laws be changed, and how often does this happen?

- ☐ Should certain laws expire over time and if so, what types?

- ☐ What is the difference between federal, state, and local government, and who has ultimate control?

- ☐ Should the government fix all problems, and why?

● ● ●

- ☐ What is welfare, and what is its goal?

- ☐ Which is more important: government assistance or private charity? Why?

- ☐ Do we need a wall or barrier around our country for protection, to keep foreigners out, or not at all, and why?

- ☐ Should everyone in America speak the same language, and why?

- ☐ Should outdated government agencies be reorganized, consolidated, or eliminated? Who should evaluate this and decide?

• • •

- ☐ Can you give examples where government is more efficient or less efficient than the private sector?

- ☐ Are all US citizens equal, and how do you know this?

- ☐ Which immigrants should we allow into our country, and why?

- ☐ What are illegal aliens, and what should be done with them?

- ☐ Should public laws take precedence over religious rules or vice versa?

• • •

- ☐ Should there be a death penalty, and why do you feel this way?

- ☐ What is Socialism, and in what country does it work best?

- ☐ What is Communism, and in what country does it work best?

- ☐ What is a dictatorship, and in what country does it work best?

- ☐ Should there be term limits for all elected officials or is this impractical?

• • •

- ☐ Should government employees receive special pension, medical, and other benefits? Why?

- ☐ Since it creates the money, are government deficits important, and why?

- ☐ Should the government spy on its own people, and how would you feel if it were watching you?

- ☐ Should government budgets be balanced, and is this important?

☐ Should the government spy on others, and does this make us safer?

● ● ●

☐ Does our country have propaganda, and can you give examples?

☐ Is Democracy the best form of government, and why?

# Questions About Business

• • •

WHETHER YOU ARE AN EMPLOYEE or an employer, understanding exactly how business works is vitally important. Unless it is a nonprofit, making money is the primary goal. Contrary to what some believe, profit is a good word. Making money is neither amoral nor unethical. Without profits, a business will eventually fail. This means providing no further goods or services, no employees, no wages, no taxes, and no Little League sponsorships. Are there any early warning signs that this is happening? If you have a business that is doing poorly, how can you turn it around and regain profitability?

Many companies start with good ideas and positive intentions. Raising funds to launch a new business can be very challenging. You must have money to make money. As strange as it sounds, banks will only loan money if you already have money (or collateral). You could look for investors, private backers, partners, or online sources like Kickstarter. Conceivably, one could also beg, borrow, and steal if necessary, but every approach has its upsides and downsides.

Once in operation, cash is king. Not simply how much is in the checkbook, but rather are you making and most importantly collecting the money? Most businesses fail due to a lack of cash. What is the revenue model, and does it generate enough to actually grow the business? If not, do you fix it by changing the model, the strategy, marketing, pricing, personnel, policies, or costs?

Writing this book may be an innovative idea. Initial costs can be covered out of pocket. Online publishing makes print and electronic copies very reasonable. But how do we market the book? Will potential readers ever find out about it? What if no one likes it? Can something like this ever become commercially successful?

A new business does not have to be unique. Think about how many plumbers, gas stations, storage lockers, cleaners, and Mexican restaurants there are. Not every model, however, works. Most of those that do succeed provide owners with a good lifestyle.

Many companies that eventually fail will do so within the first three years. Often times it takes that long to begin making any profit. Approximately 70 percent of second-generation businesses also fail, so inheriting the company still presents some elements of risk. In our country, new businesses create more jobs than older, established companies do. Surprisingly, many new businesses are actually started by immigrants.

When contemplating leaving a relatively secure job to start our first business, we debated the risk versus reward. If it did not work out, what would happen to our house, our kids, and our family? This was the biggest decision we had ever made. All of our plans for the future depended upon the outcome.

Understandably, not everyone wants to confront this kind of pressure. Few of us will ever bet the farm or go all in, but some do, and sometimes it pays off. After many years of blood, sweat, and tears, our story ended well. We started four different businesses, and all of them succeeded to varying degrees. Looking back, we would probably make the same choices all over again.

● ● ●

- ☐ Can anyone go into business, and what is necessary to start?

- ☐ How does a business work?

- ☐ How will you find a job that you like?

- ☐ Who do you feel values money more: someone who inherits it or someone who works hard for it, and why?

- ☐ How do you make money?

● ● ●

- ☐ Is it important to be on time to work, and what does this show an employer about you?

- ☐ What do you have to do to get hired?

- ☐ Why do people get fired, and who is usually at fault?

- ☐ Do most people work for the same company all of their lives? Why?

☐ Who creates jobs, and how does this happen?

● ● ●

☐ How many different jobs do you expect to have in your life, and is this a good thing?

☐ What is the difference between assets and liabilities, and which would you rather have?

☐ What is the difference between an employee and an employer, and which would you rather be?

☐ Who has more headaches: an employee or an employer? Why?

☐ What do you need to start a business?

● ● ●

☐ What is the best way for a company to get customers? What is the fastest way?

☐ What is a pro forma, and how is it developed and used?

- ☐ What is included in overhead, and how much can a company support?

- ☐ What is profit, how is it calculated, and what should be done with it?

- ☐ How long does it take a business to actually make a profit, and how are bills paid until then?

• • •

- ☐ How many years do most businesses last, and why? What is the oldest company that you know, and how has it survived so long?

- ☐ What is the minimum wage, and who should decide when to change it?

- ☐ If you want to hire someone in your business, what would you look for?

- ☐ Should government set maximum or minimum wages, and why?

- ☐ Why do some employees work harder than others do? Should everyone be paid equally?

● ● ●

- ☐ Why would you fire someone, and what would you say to him or her? How would this make you feel?

- ☐ Where could you get money to start a business?

- ☐ Do all businesses make money? Why?

- ☐ Are all business owners successful, and how can you tell?

- ☐ If a business does $1 million in sales, how much does the owner make, and what does this depend on?

● ● ●

- ☐ What do you need to get a bank loan, and what are the standard terms?

- ☐ Why do most businesses fail, and how could this have been prevented?

☐ How can you tell if a business is making money?

☐ What is embezzlement, and how can it be avoided or stopped?

☐ What types of business insurance is necessary?

• • •

☐ What different kinds of fees and taxes do businesses pay?

☐ Do some businesses and owners need licenses to operate, and how are these obtained?

☐ What does an accountant do, and is he or she always right?

☐ What are "the books," and how do you read an income statement and balance sheet?

☐ What is the best way to determine profits? Can they be measured by how much money is in the bank?

• • •

☐ How can you learn to run a business, and how long will it take?

☐ Over and above actual employee salaries, what kinds of payroll costs are there?

☐ Who collects and pays sales tax to the state?

☐ What is workers' compensation, and does it really benefit the company or the employee?

☐ Should a business be operated as a partnership, an LLC, a sub S corporation, or a regular corporation, and why?

• • •

☐ What is the difference between a private and a public company, and which is better?

☐ When should a company go public, and what is required to do so?

☐ What does employment-practices insurance cover, and who need this?

☐ Should company documents be prepared by a lawyer, and what type of records must be kept?

☐ What type of advertising works best, and how would you know?

• • •

☐ How many unhappy customers actually call and complain, and how should you handle them?

☐ Is it better to be a brick-and-mortar or an online business, and why?

☐ What kind of research should you do before starting or buying a business?

☐ Do you need to have a brand-new product or service to sell? Or can you make money doing something that others are already doing?

☐ What usually happens when an owner buys lots of expensive personal toys, and how would you feel about this?

• • •

☐ What kind of boss would you like to work for?

☐ Should women and men receive the same pay for doing the same work, and why?

☐ What is a nonprofit business, and how does it continue to operate?

☐ Should you buy an existing business or start one from scratch? Which costs more, and which takes longer to make money?

☐ How can you tell if a business will succeed?

● ● ●

# Extended Discussions

• • •

CONGRATULATIONS! HAVING MADE IT THIS far, you have either had some extraordinary discussions with kids or skipped ahead to see how this book ends. Well, this presents a slight problem. Even though you may have run out of our questions, the conversations should never end. Ask some of your own—or better yet, ask your kids to come up with some for you.

Below are several topics that we feel are very important. Unfortunately, we were unable to reduce any of them to simple questions. Therefore, each is presented as an opportunity for some in-depth dialogue.

And as always, we welcome your thoughts and suggestions about what else to incorporate in future editions of this book. Please contact us at:

MyQuestionsForKids@gmail.com or www.MyQuestionsForKids.com

Now that the process has been started, talking to kids will transform into talking to adults and eventually talking to grandkids or beyond. Hopefully, you have gotten some great answers, taught some important lessons, and developed intelligent and articulate adults who will later pass it on.

For each of us, what better legacy could there be?

• • •

☐ Does your child know what to do in an emergency? Have them demonstrate this to you including how to use a cell phone, what number to dial, and which information is pertinent to give out.

☐ What would you keep from your childhood and family life? What would you change?

☐ What is necessary to maintain a healthy life? Are immunizations important?

☐ Many people use drugs or alcohol. What are the risks and long-term consequences of this?

☐ Are there pros and cons of being sexually active, and when should people begin experimenting?

• • •

☐ When the time comes to live on your own, what will you need?

☐ How would you go about creating your own home?

☐ What qualities and characteristics will you look for in a life partner?

- ☐ How well should you know someone before you marry? What topics should be discussed and agreed to before taking the vows?

- ☐ How much does it cost to get married, and should couples be self-sufficient afterward?

● ● ●

- ☐ What is required to properly and adequately raise a family?

- ☐ Does a family need two parents to function well?

- ☐ How will you go about becoming a successful parent?

- ☐ What amount of debt should a family have?

- ☐ Who should be responsible for taking care of ageing parents?

● ● ●

- ☐ Even people in love occasionally fight. How can you fight fair to avoid hurting your partner or damaging the relationship?

- ☐ What causes people to break up or divorce? Is this necessarily a good or bad outcome, and what effects will it have on kids?

- ☐ What would it take to start your own business?

- ☐ Does anything need to change when going from employee to employer?

- ☐ There are many different models of successful businesses. How should you find one that will actually work?

• • •

- ☐ When considering work, play, and family, what will be your priority, and why?

- ☐ How far in advance should you begin planning for retirement to avoid becoming a burden on your kids?

- ☐ Have you written a will; signed durable power of attorney, medical power of attorney, and medical directive to physician forms; and shared your last wishes?

- ☐ What kind of legacy would you like to leave behind, and how will you achieve this?

☐ Have you made plans for your death? Where would you like to die? What should the obituary say and what should be on the tombstone?

● ● ●

## POSTSCRIPT

• • •

WELL OVER A YEAR HAS passed since we asked that first question, and many more questions have followed. Virtually every time we are together, our grandkids expect to be asked something new. They have actually contributed to and helped us create this book. The ultimate question, however, is whether this process has resulted in any significant change.

We can easily confirm that there are lots of discussions within and between our individual family units. No longer is anyone asking simple questions ("How was your day?") that elicit simple answers ("Fine."). The grandkids are much more open to dialogue. When asked questions, they provide thoughtful responses and can usually support their answers with additional information or detail. If they do not know an answer, they will say so without hesitation or embarrassment, and this opens the door to further learning.

They listen attentively and are quite willing to discuss a wide range of topics. It is quite acceptable to disagree, as long as one's point of view can be clearly explained and defended. Parents, as always, retain the right of having the final word, but we have not personally heard any of them use the catchall phrase "Because I said so!" to end a contentious discussion.

Mixed in with the family discourse, we also hear phrases like "What do you think about that?"; "How did it make you feel?"; "Could something else have been done?"; or "Did you learn anything from this?" Their kids have developed a greater self-awareness, introspection, and empathy for others. At the same time, each child is becoming more confident and perhaps even more mature.

Everyone is focused on education, and each child is simultaneously tasked with a wide variety of extracurricular activities, including sports, religious school, music, plays, art, gymnastics, and ballet. Time management is mandatory as active schedules leave little time to waste. Coincidentally, each family has established a limit on non-school-related screen time, including TV, video games, and all forms of social media. Even during the summer, all of the kids are reading books.

While family expectations are kept very high, no kids are perfect. Our grandkids occasionally make bad choices, and they are disciplined as a result. Appropriate punishments are accompanied, however, with clear disappointment but not embarrassment or humiliation. The goal after all is to provide a solid education, good self-esteem, and two strong feet to stand up on and become adults, just like their parents.

Bottom line—has our approach worked? While the result is still a few years off, all of the initial signs are quite good. We only gamble on outcomes that are fairly certain, but, our money is both literally and figuratively already on the table.

## ABOUT THE AUTHOR

• • •

Jon Pollock grew up in University City, Missouri along with two sisters, a brother, and multiple pets. While attending Washington University, Jon married Janie Shuman, an art student from Boston, Massachusetts.

After graduation Jon worked for Sachs Electric and in 1977 opened their Houston branch office. In 1983 he launched Pollock Electric with only one contract and three employees. This Houston firm grew to $20 million in sales when in 1998 Pollock helped create Integrated Electrical Services, a NYSE company. Within two years they acquired eighty-three US companies and were doing $1.6 billion in sales. Jon retired in 2001 and bought a condo in Coronado, California.

Two years later, however, he flunked retirement and started Trio Electric in Houston. This company has become a major player and was eventually purchased by his son Beau Pollock.

Jon and Janie have three kids and seven grandkids all living nearby in Houston.

Made in the USA  
San Bernardino, CA  
29 July 2017